Ma[illegible]
C. J. Walker

Making Dreams Happen

by Jordan Maxwell

Cover ©A'Lelia Bundles/Walker Family Collection/www.madamcjwalker.com; 3–4 ©A'Lelia Bundles/Walker Family Collection/www.madamcjwalker.com; 5–6 Liz Alger ©Harcourt Education Australia; 7–14 ©A'Lelia Bundles/Walker Family Collection/www.madamcjwalker.com.

Printed in Mexico

ISBN 10: 0-15-350652-0
ISBN 13: 978-0-15-350652-9

Ordering Options
ISBN 10: 0-15-350599-0 (Grade 2 On-Level Collection)
ISBN 13: 978-0-15-350599-7 (Grade 2 On-Level Collection)
ISBN 10: 0-15-357833-5 (package of 5)
ISBN 13: 978-0-15-357833-5 (package of 5)

1 2 3 4 5 6 7 8 9 10   050   15 14 13 12 11 10 09 08 07 06

Madam C.J. Walker was one of America's most inspiring and successful African American women. She often said, "I got my start by giving myself a start."

The farm where Sarah Breedlove lived with her parents

The Early Years

Madam Walker's real name was Sarah Breedlove. Sarah was born in Delta, Louisiana. She lived with her parents on a cotton farm.

By the time she was five years old, Sarah was working in the fields. She carried water, and she planted seeds for the new cotton crop.

Sarah's parents died when she was seven years old. A few years later, she and her sister went to work in Vicksburg, Mississippi. They worked for people and washed clothes.

An Amazing Dream

Sarah married young. Two years after her daughter was born, Sarah's husband died. She and her daughter then moved to St. Louis.

For seventeen years, Sarah worked washing clothes so that she had money to put her daughter through school.

Then something happened to Sarah's hair, and it started to fall out. She said she had a dream about a mixture that would make her hair grow again.

When she woke up, she decided to do experiments to make the mixture. Some of the things that she needed to make the mixture had to come from Africa, so she sent there for supplies.

Beginning Business

The mixture worked very well, and Sarah's hair grew back. She decided to sell her mixture as a hair product.

Sarah moved to Denver where she worked as a cook and saved her money. Before long, she was able to leave her job and start selling her new hair product.

Sarah then married a man named C.J. Walker. She decided to call herself Madam C.J. Walker, and she used the name for her products.

Madam Walker sold her products door to door and through mail order. She moved around the country, talking about her work. She also trained African American women to help sell her products.

Madam C.J. Walker's sales people in Ohio

In 1910, Madam Walker moved to Indianapolis. She built a factory and another training school there. She soon had five thousand women selling her products throughout the country.

Madam C.J. Walker's sales people at her National Convention in Philadelphia, 1917

Success

Madam Walker became one of the most successful women of her day. Not only was she wealthy, but she was able to provide hundreds of African American women with a way to earn money, too. Madam Walker died in 1919.

In 2005, a government committee recognized Madam C.J. Walker for her successful career, her hair products, and her work for the good of African Americans.

Think Critically

1. What was Madam C.J. Walker's real name?
2. In what part of the book did you read about Madam C.J. Walker's childhood?
3. What words would you use to describe Madam C.J. Walker?
4. Why did Madam C.J. Walker decide to make a hair product?
5. What products would you like to make and sell? Why?

Social Studies

Make a poster Look at the advertisement for Madam C.J. Walker's hair products on page 10. Choose something you would like to sell and think about who might want to buy it. Make a poster telling people why they should buy your product.

School-Home Connection Retell the most important facts about Madam Walker's life to a family member. Talk about why you think Madam C.J. Walker was so successful.

Word Count: 446